the Loring Greenough House

Enhancing community, history, culture, and horticulture.

Year In Review

The Loring Greenough House hosts and produces a wide range of events throughout the year to promote the use of the house and grounds as a center for historical, cultural and educational activities for Jamaica Plain and surrounding communities and to encourage a wide and diverse group of people to use and support the House.

Events & Activities 2017 to 2018

Get your tickets on Eventbrite before the event sells out!
Link from loring-greenough.org or Facebook for the Loring Greenough House

the
LORING
GREENOUGH
HOUSE

Events & Activities 2017 to 2018

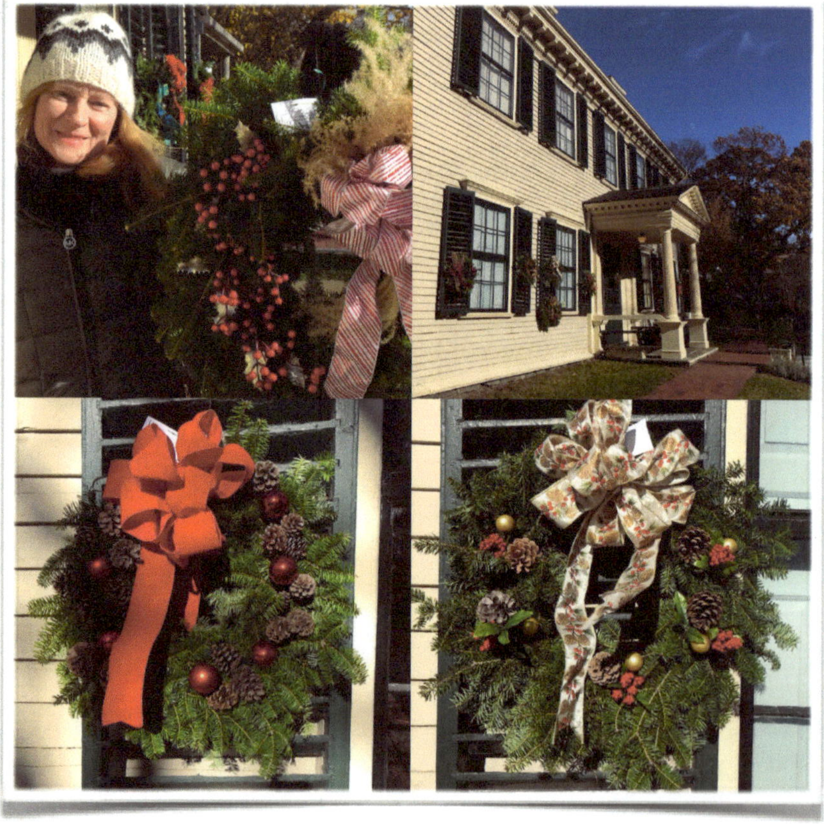

Annual Wreath Fundraiser

Events & Activities 2017 to 2018

Egg Hunt

Events & Activities 2017 to 2018

Thursdays on
the Lawn

the LORING GREENOUGH HOUSE

Events & Activities 2017 to 2018

Thursday's on the Lawn
First Thursday and Screen on the Green

Events & Activities 2017 to 2018

Chapter and Verse Literary Readings
Guided House Tours
Women In Public Art in Boston Lecture
Maria Muniz Academy performance and connections
with South Street Youth Center
Ordered signage for the trees

*Molasses
Lecture*

*Tuesday's in
the Parlor*

Events & Activities 2017 to 2018

Survey Handout during Thursday's on the Lawn
Retirement Party for Patrick & Steve from Cobwebs
Developed Sponsorship Package
Member visits to Historic Houses / Museums
Started Committee blurbs in the newsletter
Curt DiCamillo lecture

Halloween event

Events & Activities 2017 to 2018

Restore the Heart of the House

- Kitchen Cocktail fundraising party
- Crowdfunding for kitchen project

Events & Activities 2017 to 2018

Step
Inside
and
Snuggle
Up

Events & Activities 2017 to 2018

Concert Series
Summer Kitchen opening
Tuesdays in the Parlor
Book of Negroes

Weddings and Private Rentals

Events & Activities 2017 to 2018

Website launch
Annual Meeting
Ell Feasibility Study
Meeting with other local non-profits regarding CPA
funding
Appraisal day

Events & Activities 2017 to 2018

New Sub Committee - House Interiors
Punk Rock Aerobics event
History Happy Hour

Won 2nd place in the Mayor's Garden Contest.
Pride & Prejudice Party & Promenade: Joint
fundraiser with the Footlight Club.
Implemented follow up email process to the Annual
Appeal.

Events & Activities 2017 to 2018

Activated Square to collect donations
Upgraded Comcast Xfinity Modem
Installed new eero WiFi System. *Thanks eero!*
New Baking Committee
Beginning of the Master Volunteer Garden Program
New Financial System
Holiday Open House

Events & Activities 2017 to 2018

Regular e-newsletters
Acquisition of display cases and new exhibit

Apple Tree
Sponsorship
and Party

Comments From the 2017 Thursday's On The Lawn Survey:

* Love that the garden is open to the community

* Let people know a little bit about the house at Thursday's on the Lawn

* Beautiful spot and garden

* Love the Music

* Love Thursdays, bringing the community together

* Food trucks are great and want more

* Want Bigger Farmers Market

* Need more activities for different ages - teens, beer garden

Volunteer Opportunities

House Management Committee manages the historic structure of the Loring Greenough House, including preservation, rehabilitation, systems and ongoing maintenance projects. The committee seeks volunteers with interest in historic preservation, architectural history, domestic and social history, research, building maintenance and hands-on involvement. The committee meets monthly on the third Tuesday.

Landscape Committee manages the care, preservation, and advancement of our award- winning grounds of the Loring Greenough House. Volunteers are needed on all fronts, from yard care to landscape planning, with a mind to heritage cultivation and community enjoyment.

Collections Committee: Committed to preserving and presenting the art, artifacts and archives belonging to The Loring Greenough House. These objects are used in the form of curated presentations, lectures and readings. Volunteers have the opportunity to read material written and printed since the early part of the 20th century as they relate to the House. Volunteers enjoy handling practical objects such as kitchenware dating back to the last century and earlier. The Collections Committee is a great opportunity to enjoy a closer and more personal appreciation of domestic objects and artifacts from the past as well as providing an opportunity to work with archives that provide a direct telescope to seeing the past.

Programs Committee is responsible for developing and implementing dynamic events at the house throughout the year. Examples include our History Happy Hour series, movie nights, family events like the annual Egg Hunt, the Annual Garden Party, and the summertime Thursdays on the Lawn. The Committee is looking for enthusiastic, motivated people who are interested in event planning and community outreach to expand the current programming line-up.

Docent Committee interprets the House's history, collections, and architecture. Docents provide public tours. On Sundays, 1 - 3pm, April through December, at special events like First Thursdays, and by appointment. The Committee hopes to add to its roster of docents and especially seeks Spanish speakers.

Community Education Committee is an outreach group that plans events and activities designed to share the story of Loring Greenough House as well as the history of Jamaica Plain and topics of the American past with the public. The committee engages audiences through house tours, lectures and other presentations, conference attendance and field trips to other historic properties.

Development Committee: Do you enjoy planning parties, crafting letters and proposals, or saying thank you? This committee is responsible for coordinating fundraising events, managing campaigns, applying for grants, and thinking creatively about connecting the community to the Loring Greenough House through philanthropy. Together with the Programs Committee, Development is tasked with putting the word out to encourage people to join the Loring Greenough House. Members enjoy specific benefits including discounts at many events. Increasing membership is an opportunity for the LGH to have much-needed funding it can count on from year to year.

Communications Committee: Manages the communications and public relations activities with the members, sponsors, donors, media, and the public at large through written, oral, and digital means. The committee is the voice of the organization and seeks to inform and educate all its constituencies of the mission, history, community events, and successes of the Loring Greenough House.

Event Refreshment Volunteers : Do you love to bake or make appetizers? We need your help! The LGH hosts many events throughout the year and we are seeking more volunteers for refreshment-making duties! Call the house or email to get on our list!

Get involved!

Email info@loring-greenough.org
or call the house at 617-524-3158
to be connected with the appropriate committee chair!

Donors

$5,000+
Cradock Builders
James Spriggs

$2,000+
Boing Toy Store

$1,000+
Nancy Doherty, and Marcia Peters
Society of Colonial Wars

$150+
JP Licks
Whole Foods
Oriental Trading
Tillman Cooley

Fundraisers
Go Fund Me Kitchen Fundraiser
Wreath Sales
Apple Tree Sponsorship
Annual Appeal

Donate Online
http://loring-greenough.org/about-us/make-a-donation/

Volunteer Leadership

Board of Directors

Diane Spears, President

Emily Gonzalez, Vice President

Nancy Leask, Treasurer

Lorie Komlyn, Secretary

Sophy Bishop

Dorothy Clark

Michael Epp

Carol Garfield

Patricia Gilrein

Andrew Hatcher

Lorie Komlyn

Nancy Leask

Dave Nash

Diane Spears

Edward Stanley

the LORING GREENOUGH HOUSE

The Loring Greenough House
12 South Street
Jamaica Plain, MA 02130

Phone: 617.524.3158
Email: info@loring-greenough.org

Visit us on the web: loring-greenough.org

Connect Online:
facebook.com/lghouse
instagram.com/loringgreenough

Donate Online
loring-greenough.org/about-us/make-a-donation

Photos by Steve Garfield and Sarah Coyne. Book design by Steve Garfield.

Published by Steve Garfield http://stevegarfield.com © Copyright Steve Garfield 2018

www.ingramcontent.com/pod-product-compliance
Lightning Source LLC
Chambersburg PA
CBHW040254240726
48664CB00001B/391